FATS

for a healthy body

Heinemann
LIBRARY

Jillian Powell

www.heinemann.co.uk/library
Visit our website to find out more information about **Heinemann Library** books.

To order:
☎ Phone 44 (0) 1865 888066
▤ Send a fax to 44 (0) 1865 314091
▢ Visit the Heinemann Bookshop at www.heinemann.co.uk/library to browse our catalogue and order online.

First published in Great Britain by Heinemann Library, Halley Court, Jordan Hill, Oxford OX2 8EJ, part of Harcourt Education. Heinemann is a registered trademark of Harcourt Education Ltd.

Editorial: Jilly Attwood and Jennifer Tubbs
Design: Ron Kamen and Celia Floyd
Illustrations: Geoff Ward and Bob Harvey, Pennant
Picture Research: Catherine Bevan, Rosie Garai and Liz Eddison
Production: Séverine Ribierre

Originated by Ambassador Litho Ltd
Printed in China by W K T

ISBN 978 0 431 16711 4 (hardback)
07 06 05
10 9 8 7 6 5 4 3

ISBN 978 0 431 16717 6 (paperback)
08 07
10 9 8 7 6 5 4 3 2

British Library Cataloguing in Publication Data
Powell, Jillian
Fats for a healthy body
613.2'84
A full catalogue record for this book is available from the British Library.

Acknowledgements
The Publishers would like to thank the following for permission to reproduce photographs: Anthony Blake: p. **4**; Corbis: pp. **16**, **36**, **37** (Bohemian Nomad Picture Makers), **39** (Stock market/Ariel Skelley), **41** (Macduff Everton), **43**; Gareth Boden: pp. **7**, **32**; Getty Stone: pp. **29**, **33**; Liz Eddison: pp. **9**, **21**, **22**, **27**, **38**; Neil Phillips: p. **31**; Photodisc: pp. **25**, **28**; Reuters: pp. **19** (Reinhard Krause); SPL: pp. **13** (Chris Priest and Mark Clarke), **14**, **26** (Will and Deni McIntyre), **35**; Steve Behr: p. **5**; Trevor Clifford: p. **24**.

Cover photograph of butter, reproduced with permission of Gareth Boden.

Every effort has been made to contact copyright holders of any material reproduced in this book. Any omissions will be rectified in subsequent printings if notice is given to the Publishers.

Contents

Any words appearing in the text in bold, **like this**, are explained in the glossary.

Why do we need to eat?

Most people eat two or three main meals a day. We eat because we get hungry and because we enjoy the taste of food. At the same time we satisfy one of the body's essential needs – we supply it with all the chemicals it needs to stay alive and healthy.

Cells

Your body is made up of millions of tiny **cells**. For example, your bones consist of bone cells and your skin of skin cells. Most cells are so small you need a microscope to see them, but each one is working hard to carry out a particular task. To do this, your cells need a continual supply of **energy**. They also need many different chemicals, which come mainly from your food. These chemicals are called **nutrients**.

Nutrients

Carbohydrates, fats, **proteins**, **vitamins** and **minerals** are all different kinds of nutrients. Most foods contain a lot of one kind of nutrient but they contain small amounts of other nutrients too. Together nutrients provide energy, and materials that the body needs to work properly and to grow. This book is about fats, what they are and how the body uses them, but, since fats work alongside other nutrients, we shall first have a look at the part they play to make you healthy.

Whether you eat your food at home, at school or in a restaurant, you should try to eat a balanced and nutritious meal.

Energy food

Your body's main need is for food that provides energy. Everything you do uses energy, not just running and moving around, but thinking, eating, keeping warm and even sleeping. Carbohydrates and fats provide energy. The body burns carbohydrates, just like a car engine burns petrol, and it needs a big supply every day. Foods such as bread, pasta, potatoes and sugar are mainly carbohydrates and are your body's main source of energy.

Protein

Protein is needed to make new cells and repair any damaged ones. Protein is the main substance found in muscles, skin and internal **organs**. Your body is constantly renewing the cells that make up your skin, muscles and all other parts of your body. Cells consist mainly of water and protein, so to build new cells your body uses proteins that you get from foods such as meat, fish, eggs, beans and cheese. It is particularly important that children take in plenty of protein, because they are still growing and their bodies need it to make millions of extra cells.

When you do sport your body uses the energy that you get from your food.

What are fats?

It is the food we eat that helps our bodies grow, stay healthy and have **energy**. For a balanced diet, we need to eat a range of foods from three main food types: **carbohydrates**, **proteins** and fats.

Energy stores

Fats and oils are energy stores found in foods that we eat. The layer of fat which we see on a lamb chop, or as white streaks in a joint of beef, was the way the animal kept warm and stored energy. The oil that we can squeeze out of nuts and grains was the plant's energy stores. Oils are fats that are liquid at room temperature.

We eat fats in lots of different foods. We eat animal fats in meat and dairy foods, such as butter, milk and cream. We eat vegetable oils in nuts and seeds, and as liquid oils like sunflower and olive oil for frying foods or dressing salads. Fats are also used in cooked or processed foods, like cakes, biscuits, crisps, chips and pastries.

Corn oil

The oil in a seed of corn comes from inside the **germ**. If you cut a popcorn kernel in half, you can see the **husk**, **starch** and germ. The oil can be pressed out of the germ. It takes the grain from fifteen ears of corn to make fifteen millilitres of corn oil.

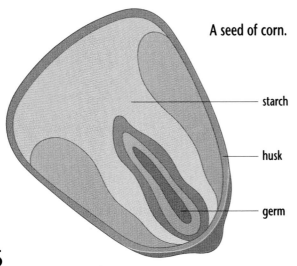

A seed of corn.

starch

husk

germ

Do you need fats?

Fats have a bad name because they are high in **kilojoules (kJ)** so they can be fattening. If you eat too many fried, fatty foods, you will increase your risk of becoming overweight or obese. But not all fats are bad for you. You need some fats in your diet to keep your body healthy.

You need fats in the diet to give you energy and help you grow. Having fats in the diet also helps your body absorb **vitamins** A, D, E and K. Fat stored in the body helps keep you warm and cushions and protects organs like your liver and kidneys.

Fatty acids

Some foods contain **fatty acids** that your body needs to stay healthy. Your body cannot make these fatty acids. You can only get them from fats that you eat. You need them to keep your brain and nerve **cells** healthy. They make skin oils and help form chemicals called **hormones** that you need for many body processes. They also help your body fight off germs and diseases and repair damaged tissue.

Fats also make food taste better, and improve its texture. Cream cakes, doughnuts and biscuits are tasty to eat.

Foods that contain fats give you lots of energy.

Fats and 'mouth feel'

Foods like bacon, burgers and chips are tempting to eat because fats add flavour and texture to food. This is what food scientists call 'mouth feel'.

What is in fats?

All the fats and oils in foods that we eat are made out of **fatty acids**. There are many different types of fatty acid, but they are all made from the same chemicals. A fatty acid is a chain of **carbon atoms**, with **oxygen** atoms attatched on one end and **hydrogen** atoms attatched on the other end.

Foods that contain fats and foods that contain **carbohydrates** both provide **energy** when we eat them. But fats are a richer source of energy than carbohydrates. Each gram of fat carries 37 **kilojoules (kJ)** of energy – over twice as many as a gram of carbohydrate does.

Fatty acids

There are over 40 different types of fatty acids in foods and about 21 in the average diet. There are three main types of fatty acids: **saturated**, **polyunsaturated**, and **monounsaturated** fatty acids. Scientists tell the different types apart by counting how many **hydrogen atoms** they have.

A **molecule** of saturated fatty acid has the maximum possible number of hydrogen atoms attached to every **carbon** atom. Scientists say it is 'saturated' with hydrogen because it can't take any more. This type of fatty acid is mainly found in animal foods like meat and cream.

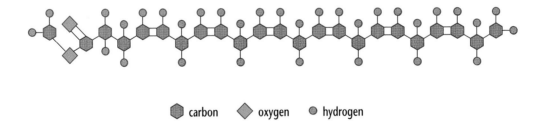

⬡ carbon   ◆ oxygen   ● hydrogen

A fatty acid chain in a molecule of an **unsaturated** fat.
A whole molecule is made up of three chains.

Fat fish fact
Cold-water fish like tuna and salmon are high in polyunsaturated fats. If they were high in saturated fat, which is solid in cold temperatures, they would freeze solid in icy water!

Find the fats

A sample of food can be tested for fats by shaking it in **ethanol**, which is a type of alcohol. Any fats **dissolve** in the ethanol. This **solution** can then be poured into water. Fats are **insoluble** in water so tiny droplets of fats will form in water if they are present. A simpler test of fats is to press a sample of food between two sheets of paper. Fats and oils will leave a greasy mark on the paper.

Some fatty acids are missing one pair of hydrogen atoms in the middle of the molecule. There is one gap or 'unsaturation', so they are called monounsaturated fatty acids. ('Mono' means one.) They are found in foods like olive oil and peanuts. Other fatty acids are missing more than one pair of hydrogen atoms. They are called polyunsaturates. ('Poly' means many.) They are found in vegetable oils like sunflower oil.

Saturated fats like butter and lard have a melting temperature of at least 20° Celsius so they are solid at room temperature. Monounsaturated fats like olive oil are liquid at room temperature but turn cloudy and begin to thicken when they are kept in cold temperatures. Polyunsaturated fats like sunflower oil always remain liquid, however cold the temperature.

Fats can be solid or liquid depending on the type of fatty acids they contain.

9

How do we get fats from food?

When you eat foods containing fats, your body needs to break the fats down so it can use them for **energy** and other body needs. Fats are broken down by your **digestive system**.

Eating and digesting

First you chew food, mashing it up and mixing it with **saliva** so it is softer and easier to swallow. Then the food passes down the oesophagus into your stomach where stomach acids and **enzymes** start to break it down. Enzymes are a kind of **protein**. Their job is to speed up **chemical reactions** in **cells**.

Your stomach begins to digest proteins from your food, then passes it on to your small intestine. The small intestine's job is to break food down into **soluble** particles that can be absorbed into your blood.

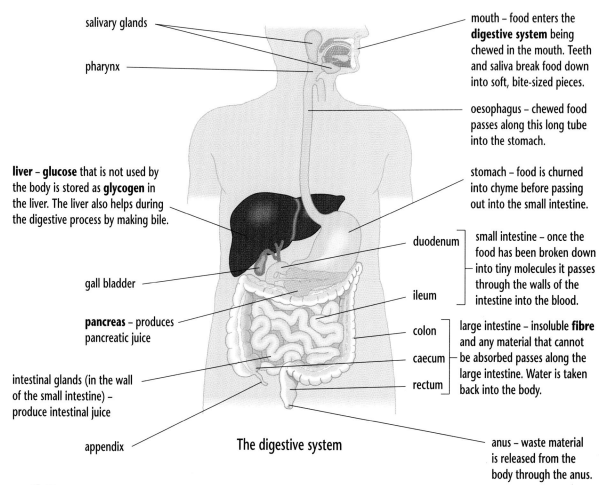

salivary glands

pharynx

liver – **glucose** that is not used by the body is stored as **glycogen** in the liver. The liver also helps during the digestive process by making bile.

gall bladder

pancreas – produces pancreatic juice

intestinal glands (in the wall of the small intestine) – produce intestinal juice

appendix

duodenum

ileum

colon

caecum

rectum

mouth – food enters the **digestive system** being chewed in the mouth. Teeth and saliva break food down into soft, bite-sized pieces.

oesophagus – chewed food passes along this long tube into the stomach.

stomach – food is churned into chyme before passing out into the small intestine.

small intestine – once the food has been broken down into tiny molecules it passes through the walls of the intestine into the blood.

large intestine – insoluble **fibre** and any material that cannot be absorbed passes along the large intestine. Water is taken back into the body.

anus – waste material is released from the body through the anus.

The digestive system

Emulsification

You can watch emulsification happening to fats by pouring water into a greasy pan. A layer of fat will rise to the top of the water. If you add a few drops of washing-up liquid, the fat will begin to emulsify and break down into smaller droplets.

First of all the fats have to be broken down so they are small enough to be absorbed. Fats are **insoluble** in water, so, a substance called **bile** does the job of breaking up fats from foods so they can dissolve in water. Bile is made by the liver and stored in the gall bladder. After a meal, bile is released and passes into the small intestine where it begins breaking up the fats you have just eaten. This process is called **emulsification** and bile mixes with the fat breaking the large fat droplets into smaller droplets. This makes it easier for your body to absorb it.

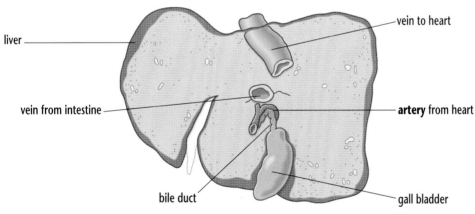

liver — vein to heart — vein from intestine — **artery** from heart — bile duct — gall bladder

A cross section of the liver.

Fat stores

Your body can absorb and store fat in its liver, muscle and fat cells. Fat cells make up fat tissue, which is found under the skin and cushioning internal organs like the liver and kidneys. In liver and muscle cells, fat is stored as microscopic droplets of fat. You can see these tiny droplets of fat in an animal's muscles as white streaks on meat.

How does the body absorb fats?

Absorbing fats

Once the **bile** has **emulsified** (broken down) the fats, your body needs to absorb them. Your **pancreas** sends out **enzymes** which attack the fat **molecules**. They break them down into **fatty acids** and **glycerol**. These are substances that can be absorbed into the cells that line your intestines.

Inside the **cells** of the small intestine, the fatty acids and glycerol are re-built into bundles of fat **molecules** called **triglycerides**. These fatty molecules have a **protein** coating which makes the fat **dissolve** more easily in water. They are now able to pass into your **lymphatic system**. Your lymphatic system uses liquids to carry substances around your body, and get rid of waste matter and **toxins**. From the lymphatic system, fats can pass into your hepatic portal vein to the **liver** and then into your bloodstream.

Your body now needs to absorb the fats being carried in your bloodstream into its fat, muscle and liver cells where it can use or store them as **energy**. It uses enzymes to break them down into fatty acids again. These enzymes are triggered by a **hormone** or chemical called **insulin**.

All of your body needs fat for energy

Your body needs to move fat to different parts, either to be used as energy, or to be stored for later use. The fat molecules need to be broken into fatty acids because these smaller particles can move between cells across the cell wall. However, when the body needs to transport fat around the body in the blood or in the lymph system, fatty acids are not the most efficient way. Lots of fatty acids attract lots of water which would take more energy up, but fewer large fat molecules attract less water and use up less energy.

What is insulin?

Insulin is a hormone made in the body by the **pancreas**. It does an important job in helping your body build its energy stores. When you eat a meal or sweet snack, your body detects fatty acids, **amino acids** and **glucose** in your intestine. Your brain tells your pancreas to produce insulin. Insulin works on many cells in the body, especially your liver, muscles and fat cells. It encourages them to absorb fatty acids, glucose and amino acids and to start using them to build your body's energy stores.

If levels of insulin in the body are high, the enzymes are very active. If levels of insulin are low, they are not active. The enzymes break down the fats in your blood into fatty acids and glycerol which can be absorbed and stored in your liver, muscle and fat cells. Inside these cells, insulin encourages them to form molecules of fat. These fat molecules are an important part of your body's energy stores.

People with diabetes can inject the insulin that their bodies need.

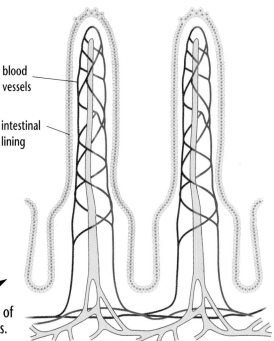

When insulin goes wrong

Your body makes insulin when you eat. Normally, it can make all the insulin you need, but sometimes, the body may not be making enough insulin. This is called **diabetes**. People who are diabetic may need to inject insulin.

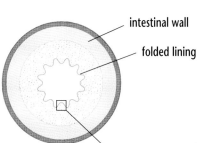

intestinal wall

folded lining

Detail of intestinal lining.

internal surface covered by villi

Detail of a villus.

blood vessels

intestinal lining

The large surface area of the villi helps the absorption of fats in the intestine.

How does the body store fat?

Fat is stored in tissue called 'adipose tissue'. It is made up of fat **cells**. Fat cells are like tiny plastic bags that hold a droplet of fat inside. There are two types of fat cells: white fat and brown fat. White fat cells are large cells. They contain one large fat droplet. Brown fat cells are smaller. They contain several smaller fat droplets.

White fat is important for giving your body warmth, **energy** and protective cushioning. Brown fat is found mainly in newborn babies, between their shoulders, and is important for keeping them warm.

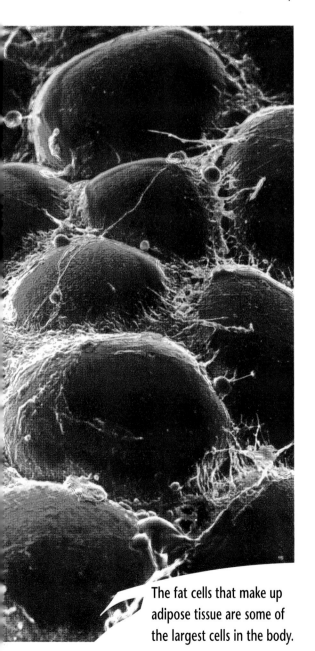

The fat cells that make up adipose tissue are some of the largest cells in the body.

Babies and brown fat

Fat cells form in an unborn baby in the last three months of pregnancy. Newborn babies do not have much white fat stored, so they make warmth by breaking down the fat **molecules** in brown fat cells. Once babies start to eat more and grow, white fat begins to be stored in their white fat cells and replaces the brown fat. Adults have few or no brown fat cells. After **puberty**, the body makes no more fat cells. As it stores more fat, the number of fat cells remains the same but the cells get bigger.

Some body fat is stored under your skin. It is important for keeping you warm because it does not allow heat to pass through it very easily. Fat also cushions and protects your internal **organs** such as your kidneys.

Your body's fat cells are much less active than other cells. They don't metabolize fat; they just store it. When you eat a meal containing fats, your fat cells pick up spare fat in your bloodstream and store it.

Fat is the most energy dense of all the macronutrients. Fat provides 37 **kilojoules** per gram, whereas **protein** provides 17 kilojoules, **carbohydrate** provides 16 kilojoules and alcohol provides 29 kilojoules. If we consume more energy than we use up, the excess energy is stored as fat. This is why eating to many fatty foods, which provided lots of energy, may lead to weight gain.

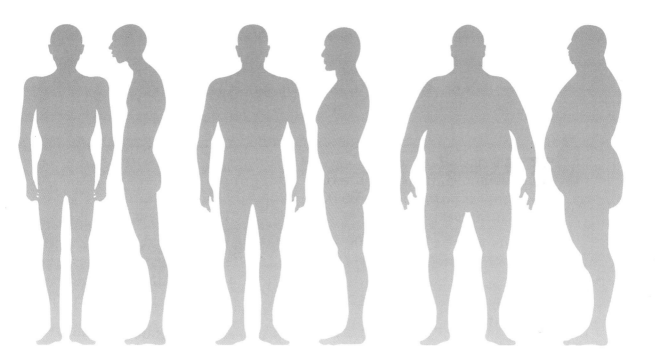

There are three main body types. From left to right they are: ectomorph (lean and delicate), mesomorph (compact and muscular) and endomorph (fat).

Body Mass Index
The Body Mass Index (BMI) can be calculated as follows:

$$\frac{\text{weight in kilograms}}{(\text{height in metres})^2}$$

This calculation can be used to assess the degree to which an adult is overweight. A BMI of below 17.5 is underweight, 17.5 – 24.9 is desirable, 25 – 29.5 is overweight and 30 and above is considered **obese**.

How does the body get energy from fats?

Your body gets **energy** from the food you eat. It can get energy from foods containing fats, **carbohydrates** and **proteins**. For a healthy diet, you need to take energy from different food sources. Fats are the richest source of energy. They provide twice as much energy per gram as carbohydrates or proteins do. We measure the energy we take from food in **kilojoules**.

Compare the energy
- 1 gram of fat provides 37 kilojoules of energy
- 1 gram of carbohydrate provides 16 kilojoules of energy
- 1 gram of protein provides 17 kilojoules of energy.

When we are active our bodies burn fat like cars burn fuel.

Why do you need energy?

Your body needs energy just to keep warm. You need energy for basic body processes like breathing and digesting food and even sleeping. Young people need extra energy for growing. Your body is using energy even when you are resting. It uses energy to grow new cells and repair damaged cells.

The amount of energy you are using each minute when you are resting is called your **basal metabolic rate (BMR)**. An adult uses around 4.6 kilojoules of energy for basic body processes each minute. Men have higher BMRs than women because they have more muscle to work. Older people tend to have lower BMRs because they have lost some of their muscle with ageing. Infants and young children have a high BMR because they are using energy to grow. The basal metabolic rate accounts for about three-quarters of our total energy needs. The rest of our energy needs depends on our body weight and how active we are.

You need to take in enough energy from your food to stay a healthy weight for your size and give you energy for activities. You could run all day just on chocolate bars, but although they would give you energy, they would not provide the other **nutrients** you need from your diet. In **developed countries**, fats provide around 40 per cent of the energy we take from our food. But health experts recommend that fats should provide no more than 35 per cent of our total energy intake – around 78 grams of fat if 8370 kilojoules are consumed. We should take about 50 per cent of our energy from starchy carbohydrates and the rest from proteins.

How much do you need?
The energy you need depends on your age and how active you are. A baby boy just under a year old needs about 3850 kilojoules of energy a day. A baby girl needs about 3619 kilojoules of energy a day. By the time they are aged between eleven and fourteen, the boy needs about 9290 kilojoules of energy a day and the girl needs about 7720 kilojoules of energy a day.

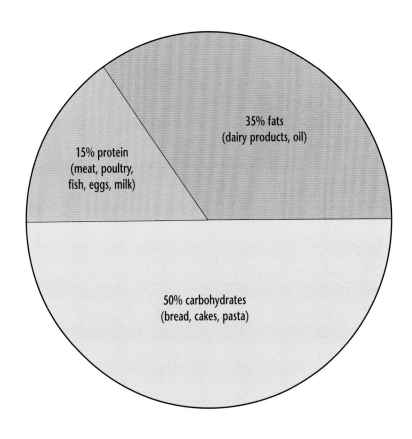

35% fats
(dairy products, oil)

15% protein
(meat, poultry,
fish, eggs, milk)

50% carbohydrates
(bread, cakes, pasta)

The chart shows the percentages of total energy intake that should come from fats, carbohydrates and protein.

How does the body turn fats into energy?

The more active you are, the more **energy** your body needs. When you are resting, your body is using just a few **kilojoules** each minute. Between meals, it can use **fatty acids** from your bloodstream as well as **glucose** to give you energy. When you start to become active, you will need more energy. Walking quickly, you will use between 10 and 15 kilojoules each minute. Playing a sport or running, you will use around 30 to 40 kilojoules each minute.

Where does the energy come from?

As you become more active, your body begins to take energy from glucose (blood sugar) in your blood. Glucose is the body's main source of energy. Some **cells** in your body, like your brain cells, can only get energy from glucose. Glucose is made from **carbohydrate** foods that you eat and then stored in your **liver** as **glycogen**.

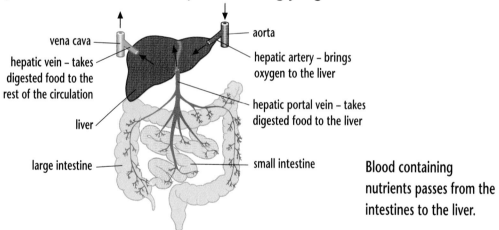

vena cava

hepatic vein – takes digested food to the rest of the circulation

liver

large intestine

aorta

hepatic artery – brings oxygen to the liver

hepatic portal vein – takes digested food to the liver

small intestine

Blood containing nutrients passes from the intestines to the liver.

The liver acts like a chemical factory unlocking energy from your food. A vein carries blood containing food **nutrients** from the intestine to the liver. The liver sorts through the blood. It removes chemical waste and stores useful substances like glucose and vitamins.

Energy for exercise

As you exercise, your body draws on stored carbohydrates and fats to give you energy. It first takes energy from muscle glycogen, which it has stored from starchy carbohydrate foods. The body can only store a certain amount of glycogen. The bigger your muscles are the more glycogen they can hold.

When you are resting or performing light activities such as walking or writing, your body mainly metabolizes fat as a source of energy for your muscles. When you start to exercise the working muscles need a more immediate source of energy so the body switches from using fat to stored glycogen as the source of energy. Once all the glycogen has been used up you start to feel tired and are forced to slow down as the muscles can only use fat for energy.

A trained athlete's body burns fat more quickly than a normal person's body. The longer and harder they exercise, the more fat is burned for energy. After an hour's hard exercise, up to 75 per cent of their energy may be provided by fats.

How much energy?

An adult uses an average of 10,041 kilojoules of energy each day, depending on how active he or she is. A young man will use around 6 kilojoules of energy each minute just sitting down. Walking slowly, he will use around 13 kilojoules of energy each minute. If he plays football, the energy he uses will increase to 30 kilojoules each minute.

Fat activity

Your body metabolizes fat to give it energy. If you hold a peanut over a flame, the fat it contains will start to burn as it gives off energy as heat. When you eat a peanut, your body digests the fat, which will be stored or used as energy.

Athletes who compete all over the world use a lot of energy every day.

Fats for vitamins

You need some fats in your diet because they provide you with the **vitamins** A, D, E and K that you need to stay healthy. All these vitamins are **fat-soluble**, which means they are **dissolved** in the fats in your food. They are found in foods such as meat, liver, dairy foods, egg yolks, vegetable seed oils and leafy green vegetables. Some foods, such as milk and margarine, have vitamins A and D added to them. If you ate a very low fat diet for a long time, your body might not get enough of these important vitamins. When you digest foods containing fats, fat-soluble vitamins are carried into the intestine, where your body can absorb them.

Vitamin A

Vitamin A is found in oily fish, fish liver oils, liver, eggs, dairy products and some vegetables like carrots. Your body needs it for growth, healthy skin and good eyesight. A shortage, or deficiency, of vitamin A can result in problems with eyesight and even blindness. Your body can only absorb vitamin A by taking it from fats in foods that you eat. You can get vitamin A from animal or vegetable foods. Animal sources of vitamin A are six times stronger than vegetable sources, and can be toxic if you have too much.

Vitamin A deficiency
The World Health Organization estimates that between 100 and 140 million children in developing countries suffer from vitamin A deficiency. It is a problem in 118 countries, especially in Africa and South-east Asia. It can cause blindness and result in death and disease from infections, especially for children and pregnant women. The World Health Organization runs programmes to give liquid vitamin A to children while they are being **immunized** against other diseases such as polio.

The sunshine vitamin

Vitamin D is sometimes called the sunshine vitamin because sunlight is one source of it for your body. It is also found in liver, oily fish, fish liver oils, margarine and fortified breakfast cereals. Vitamin D is important for forming healthy bones and a deficiency can result in bone problems such as rickets. This is a disease which means bones do not grow well.

Vitamin E

You need vitamin E for healthy skin and it is also important for long term health. It is found in eggs, liver, butter, milk, nuts, vegetable oils and seeds.

Vitamin K

Vitamin K is important for healthy blood and circulation. It is found in green vegetables, tomatoes, eggs and some cereals.

Vitamin stores

Your body can store fat-soluble vitamins in your **liver** and in your fat **cells**, until it needs them. You can top up your vitamin stores by eating more of the right kinds of food. Some groups of people like pregnant women, growing children and the elderly may need extra vitamins, but it is important not to take in too many fat-soluble vitamins because they can build up in the liver and have **toxic** effects.

These foods are part of a healthy diet because they contain essential **fatty acids** and vitamins.

Essential fatty acids

Your body can convert **fatty acids** from foods into different types of fatty acids to be used in different **cells** as it needs them. But there are two kinds of **polyunsaturated fatty acids** (**PUFAs**) that your body cannot make, which are essential for your health. These are called **essential fatty acids** (**EFAs**) and you can only get them by eating foods that contain them. They are linoleic acid, found in vegetable seed oils such as sunflower oil, soya oil and in small amounts in animal fats, such as fatty meat. The second EFA is linolenic acid, found in small amounts in vegetable oils.

Polyunsaturated fatty acids (PUFAs)

Scientists group PUFAs into two families, called **Omega 3 fatty acids** and **Omega 6 fatty acids**. They tell these fatty acids apart by looking at the chain of **carbon** and **hydrogen atoms** and finding out at which position along the chain the first missing hydrogen atom occurs. If the first missing hydrogen occurs at carbon atom number 3, the PUFA belongs to the Omega 3 family; if the first missing hydrogen occurs at carbon atom number 6, the PUFA belongs to the Omega 6 family.

Foods like oily fish, nuts and leafy green vegetables are all sources of fat-soluble **vitamins**.

Polyunsaturated fatty acids are found in fresh foods such as oily fish, green leafy vegetables, seeds and nuts, beans, and grains. The Omega 6 group are found in vegetable oils such as sunflower oil and margarines. The Omega 3 group are found in soybeans, walnuts, linseed and flax oil, dark green leafy vegetables and oily fish like tuna and mackerel. Linoleic acid belongs to the Omega 6 family, linolenic acid belongs to the Omega 3 family of PUFAs.

Why do you need EFAs?

Many types of body cell, including your brain, nerve, skin, and hair cells need EFAs to keep them healthy. They are also needed to help your body make **hormones**. EFAs are also important for the body's **immune system**, which defends the body against infections by **bacteria** and **viruses**.

How much fat do we need in our diets?

Current recommendations for fatty acid intake are that, on average, total fat and saturates should provide not more than 35 per cent and 11 per cent, respectively, of dietary **energy** intake. **Monounsaturates** should provide 13 per cent of dietary energy. **Polyunsaturates** should provide 6.5 per cent of energy and a daily intake of 0.2 grams (1.5 grams per week) Omega 3 polyunsaturates is also recommended. The essential fatty acids, linoleic acid and alpha linoleic acid should provide at least 1 per cent and 0.2 per cent respectively, of dietary energy.

Although not essential, other Omega 3 fatty acids may help protect you against heart disease by keeping your blood flowing smoothly, and may also keep your joints healthy and protect you against diseases like arthritis.

Storing Fatty Acids

Fatty acids react easily with chemicals in the body, which is why they have health-giving powers. But this also means they can make foods containing them change chemically, so nuts and seeds can spoil or become stale when the fats in them oxidise (react with oxygen in the air). They need to be kept cool and stored in an airtight container.

Fats in processed foods

Foods like seeds and grains contain natural **fatty acids**. When we eat them, we also take in **fibre** which the body needs to help keep the bowel healthy, and **antioxidant vitamins** which it needs to keep **cells** healthy.

However, some fatty acids are chemically changed when food is processed. Fats are used in many processed foods such as cooking oils and spreads, cakes, and ready-made meals. Manufacturers process natural foods to get the look and taste they want. They heat the food and use chemicals called **additives** to change the colour, texture, taste and smell.

Hydrogenated fats

One of these processes is called **hydrogenation**. It is used to turn **unsaturated** fats, which are liquid at room temperature, into a solid form for margarines, spreads and cooking fats. It also makes fats less likely to spoil while foods are being stored. Hydrogenated fats are used to make crisp chips and tasty doughnuts.

Cakes are often made using hydrogenated fat.

These fats can appear on food labels as 'hydrogenated fat', 'partially hydrogenated fat', 'hardened fat', 'vegetable fat', 'vegetable suet' or 'margarine'. Hydrogenated fats may also be used for frying foods like chips.

Hydrogenation means adding **hydrogen** into fatty acid chains so they become **'saturated'** with hydrogen. Hydrogenation changes some of the unsaturated fats into saturated fats. The rest become **trans fats**. Trans fats help fats pack closely together so they stay solid at room temperature, like a margarine spread.

Trans fats

Natural trans fats are sometimes found in small amounts in foods such as meat and dairy foods. But most trans fats come from fried foods and high-fat processed foods such as margarines, spreads, doughnuts, cakes and crackers.

A high level of trans fats in the diet has undesirable effects on blood **cholesterol** levels, by causing an increase in **LDL cholesterol** levels and a decrease in **HDL cholesterol** levels. This can increase the risk of heart disease. The present average intake of trans fats in the UK is about 5 grams per day or 2 per cent of dietary energy. Current recommendations are that trans fats should provide no more than 2 per cent of dietary **energy**. This target has been helped by many manufacturers removing trans fats from their products.

Frying fat

Fats can also change chemically when they are heated at high temperatures. Frying can make some cooking oils **oxidize** (react with oxygen) and create chemicals called **free radicals** which can damage and age body cells. Butter and olive oil are less likely to oxidize at high temperatures.

Fats can change chemically when they are heated at high temperatures.

Fat and cholesterol

Cholesterol is a type of fat found in your body. Your body needs some cholesterol to build **cell** walls and brain and nerve tissue. It also uses cholesterol to make **hormones** needed for basic processes like digestion. Your body can make about 75 per cent of the cholesterol it needs from the dietary fat that you eat. One of the things cholesterol is used for is to be converted into **bile** acids which help digest and absorb fat from the diet.

Dietary cholesterol

You also take in some cholesterol from your diet. Dietary cholesterol is found in animal foods, such as egg yolks, meat, liver, some shellfish and milk. Unless you have a very high intake, dietary cholesterol has little effect on cholesterol levels in your blood. Blood cholesterol levels are mainly affected by intake of **saturates**.

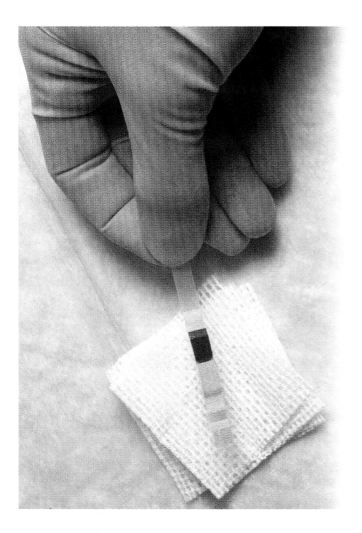

Blood cholesterol levels

Good cholesterol molecules (called **HDL cholesterol)** help carry cholesterol and fats away from the **arteries** to the **liver** where they can be safely broken down. HDL cholesterol can help protect the body against heart disease. But, bad cholesterol molecules (called **LDL cholesterol**) can slowly build up in the walls of the arteries that feed blood to the heart and brain. It can start to form fatty deposits that clog the arteries. If a **blood clot** forms, it can block the flow of blood and **oxygen** to the heart muscle and cause a heart attack. It if blocks the flow of blood and oxygen to the brain it can cause a **stroke**.

A blood cholesterol test shows the level of cholesterol present in the blood.

Controlling cholesterol

Doctors measure the amount of cholesterol in the blood in millimoles per litre of blood (mmol/l). They recommend that blood cholesterol should be kept below 5.0 mmol/l to help prevent heart disease. Diets in countries like the USA and the UK, which are high in animal foods, can often lead to high blood cholesterol. This increases the risk of heart disease so doctors recommend reducing blood cholesterol by changes in diet and lifestyle.

Lowering cholesterol

Blood cholesterol levels can be lowered by reducing the intake of saturates from the diet. Replacing saturates with **monounsaturates** and **polyunsaturates** can help lower LDL cholesterol and raise or maintain HDL cholesterol levels. Other foods such as porridge oats, which contain **soluble fibre**, may also help reduce blood cholesterol levels. There are also some food products like yoghurts and margarine spreads that can help lower blood cholesterol. They contain a plant ingredient called plant stanol ester, which stops the body absorbing dietary cholesterol.

Low fat foods can help control the amount of dietary cholesterol. Some foods can even help reduce cholesterol in the body.

Control cholesterol by:
- losing excess weight
- taking more exercise
- stopping smoking
- reducing alcohol intake
- avoiding too many foods high in saturates
- eating a low fat diet
- eating foods that contain fibre e.g. fruits, vegetables, whole grains and cereals.

Fats and over-eating

When you take in more **energy** than you use up the excess energy is stored as fat and can lead you to become overweight. Foods containing a lot of fat provide more energy than those that contain mainly either **carbohydrate** or **protein**. People like high fat foods such as burgers and chips, cakes and doughnuts, because their fat content gives them a nice taste and 'mouth-feel'; this is what can tempt people to over-eat.

Obesity

A recent survey of adults in the United Kingdom showed that 45 per cent of men and 33 per cent of women were overweight, and 19 per cent of men and 21 per cent of women were **obese**. Being obese carries a much greater risk of developing diseases such as **diabetes**, heart disease, high blood pressure and some cancers. Therefore, these people should be encouraged to lose weight. Weight may be lost by decreasing energy intake and increasing physical activity. The best way to decrease energy intake is to avoid eating too many energy-dense foods, which tend to be high in fat.

Scientists are studying the effects of how a 'fat **gene**' may cause obesity.

Fat and the basal metabolic rate

Fat **cells** are not as active as other body cells, such as muscle cells. They use a lot less energy than muscle cells. So, the more fat and less muscle the body carries, the lower the **basal metabolic rate** (see page 16) of that person will be.

When a person wants to lose weight they should reduce their energy intake and become more active so that they are using up more energy than they are taking in. People wanting to lose weight should not reduce their energy intake by too much or they will start to lose muscle as well as fat. It is important that people who are dieting get a good intake of all the essential **nutrients**, therefore, the diet should be high in fruit and vegetables and include high **fibre**, low fat foods.

Obesity is a growing problem in many parts of the developed world.

A person can increase both their basal metabolic rate and their overall metabolic rate through exercise and physical activity. Exercises which develop muscle, such as weight training or jobs which involve lifting and carrying, mean that the body will be using up more energy even at rest. Activities such as walking, running, dancing and playing sport are called **cardiovascular** and use up a lot of energy whilst you are doing them. Running for 30 minutes can use up to 300 kcals. This is why experts recommend a combination of exercises and activities for weight loss.

Fats and obesity

We need to eat just enough fats to keep our body healthy and give us **energy**. If we are active and get lots of exercise, our body will use the fats we eat to give it energy. By balancing our energy intake and output, we will stay a healthy weight.

Fat rats!

In a study at the University of Illinois, USA, one group of rats was fed a diet of 42 per cent fats (the average fat intake for people in **developed countries**). The other group was fed on a low fat diet. Both groups were given as much to eat as they wanted. After 60 weeks, the low fat group was still lean and sleek. The high fat group were overweight and had up to 51 per cent body fat.

Body mass index

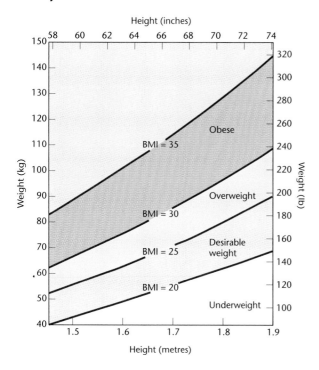

Work out your BMI from the chart or use the formula

BMI = Weight in kg ÷ (height in m)^2

A BMI of less than 20 is underweight
20–24.9 is desirable
25–29.9 is overweight
30+ is obese

Fat lifestyles

It is normal to store fat when you are growing in infancy and adolescence. But the diet and lifestyle we have today mean that many children and adults are overweight. Popular foods like burgers and chips, pastries and ice cream are high in fat. Many processed foods carry hidden fats. Also, people get much less exercise than they used to. In your great-grandparents' day, many people used to walk and cycle to work and school. Now many people go by car or public transport. In the past, people were more active in their leisure time, too. Now they spend more time sitting down and watching television or using computers. Even central heating stops us using energy to keep us warm. Sitting in a warm room watching television uses as little energy as sleeping!

Obesity

More people are becoming **obese**. People are classified as obese when they have a BMI of 30 or above. In the UK, one in five adults are obese. Doctors think that by 2010, this will rise to one in four. A third of obese adults were obese as children. Between 5 and 15 per cent of British school children are overweight and likely to grow into obese adults. The main causes of obesity are poor diet and lack of exercise.

Scientists are researching drugs to fight obesity, but the best way of tackling it is to reduce the amount of kilojoules eaten each day, eat a low fat diet and take more exercise.

Keep fit not fat

Regular exercise helps burn off fat stores and it may also speed up the **metabolic rate** – the rate at which the body turns food into energy – by up to ten times.

Exercise keeps your body healthy, and it can be lots of fun.

Fats and health problems

Fats should make up no more than 35 per cent of our diet. This will give us plenty of **energy** and all our **essential fatty acids**. But the diet in **developed countries** such as the UK or the USA, which contains lots of fatty products, can take approximately 40 per cent of total energy intake from fats.

Health problems

A high fat diet can cause many health problems. Some of these are linked with **obesity**. Obesity increases the risk of coronary heart disease, **stroke**, **diabetes** and some cancers. Doctors believe that an 'apple' body shape, which carries most fat around the middle is more at risk from health problems than a 'pear' shape, which carries most weight around the hips and thighs.

Obesity puts extra stress on many parts of the body, such as the bones, blood circulation and nerves. It increases the risk of osteo-arthritis, where the joints become painful and swollen. It also increases the risk of diabetes, which means the body does not produce enough **insulin** or use it properly. Obesity can also lead to high blood pressure, heart and breathing problems and some types of cancer.

Saturated fats are found in:
- meat and dairy food
- some plant oils, like coconut and palm oil
- processed foods like cakes, biscuits, chips and crisps.

Chips might be tasty, but if you eat them too often you will run the risk of damaging your health.

Cancer

Diets that are high in fat, especially saturates, have been directly linked with some cancers, including cancer of the breast, colon and skin.

Doctors believe about 30 to 40 per cent of all cancers could be prevented by eating a diet that is low in fat and high in **fibre** and taking regular exercise. They recommend diets that are low in fat and high in plant foods, such as fresh fruits and vegetables to prevent cancer. You should aim to eat at least five portions of a variety of fruit and vegetables every day. This includes canned, frozen and dried types as well as fresh.

Cancer facts

Women in Japan have low rates of breast cancer compared to women in the west. They eat a diet that is low in saturates, and high in fish oils and soy **protein**. When Japanese women move to the west and eat a western diet, their rate of breast cancer increases.

You can reduce your intake of saturates by choosing lean meat and removing visible fat or skin on meat where possible, and by choosing low fat dairy products such as semi-skimmed milk and reduced fat cheese. You can also avoid eating too many fatty meat products, cakes, biscuits and pastries.

Sushi – often made with raw fish – is a popular part of the Japanese diet.

Fats and heart disease

Eating too many saturates in the diet increases the risk of heart disease. Heart disease causes 40 per cent of all deaths in the USA and Europe!

Blocking arteries

Having a high intake of **saturates** in the diet raises the level of **cholesterol** in the blood. The cholesterol can accumulate in the walls of the vessels in the heart. Once it starts to build up it can oxidize and cause the vessels to 'fur up' and become narrow as the overgrowth in the vessel walls becomes a hardened plaque. This leads to a reduced flow of blood to the heart and may cause chest pain (angina), particularly during exercise.

As the fats and cholesterol build up, they gather calcium which starts to harden the **artery** walls. This thickening and hardening of the artery walls is called arteriosclerosis. It can be caused by:
- eating too many saturates
- having high levels of blood cholesterol
- smoking
- not getting enough exercise
- being **obese**
- having high blood pressure
- having **diabetes**.

artery wall

fat deposits

Artery walls can become blocked by fat deposits.

Sources of saturated fats in the UK diet:
22 per cent from meats and meat products
22 per cent from oils and spreads
27 per cent from dairy products like milk and cheese
11 per cent from cakes, biscuits and pastries
18 per cent other foods – soups, sauces, sweets.
(Source of information: British Nutrition Foundation.)

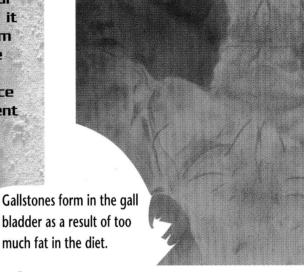

What are gallstones?

Your **liver** makes bile to help you break down fats in your food. But if you eat too many fatty foods, your liver can begin to produce too much **bile**. Bile can then build up in your gall bladder. As it builds up, it can start to harden and form gallstones. These can cause pain and may need surgery. Low fat diets can help reduce cholesterol levels and prevent gallstones building up.

Gallstones form in the gall bladder as a result of too much fat in the diet.

Angina and heart attack

As the arteries get thicker and harder, it is more difficult for blood to flow round the body. When someone starts to exercise, their heart has to work harder to try and pump blood to their muscles. They can start to get pains in their legs because the muscles are not getting enough blood and **oxygen**. They can also get pain around the heart muscle if it is not getting enough blood and oxygen. This heart pain is called angina.

Eventually, the thick, sticky blood can form a **blood clot** which blocks an artery. If it blocks an artery that leads to the heart, it can cause a heart attack. If it blocks an artery leading to the brain, it can cause a **stroke**.

Don's story

Don Salmon was in his early sixties and had just retired from his job as a lorry driver when he suffered a heart attack. Don used to be a smoker and enjoyed a breakfast of bacon, eggs and fried bread every day. Doctors found he had a high blood cholesterol level. They recommended that he cut out red meat, eat no more than three eggs a week and use low fat dairy products. This has helped Don reduce the risk of another heart attack.

Fats preventing disease

A high intake of **saturates** and **trans fats** can both raise blood **cholesterol** levels and lead to heart disease. But some **unsaturates** may help protect against heart disease by lowering bad cholesterol and raising or maintaining good cholesterol in the blood.

The good fats

Monounsaturates, such as olive oil and **polyunsaturates**, such as sunflower oil, may lower blood cholesterol levels. They also provide vitamin E, which may protect against heart disease. Nuts, especially walnuts and almonds, are also rich in polyunsaturated **fatty acids** which can protect against heart disease and lower blood cholesterol. Monounsaturates may also increase levels of the good **HDL cholesterol**, and so help protect against heart disease.

Patients recovering from a heart attack are advised to eat a healthier diet.

Diets across the world

The diet typically eaten in northern Europe and the USA contains high levels of saturates, from meat and dairy foods, and also from cooking by roasting or frying. In other parts of the world, including Asia and Africa, meat is only used to add flavour and texture to a meal, or is saved for special occasions. Cooking is based on starchy **carbohydrates**, such as rice and couscous, eaten with pulses and vegetables. Low levels of saturated fats are linked with lower rates of heart disease.

The Mediterranean diet

Mediterranean countries such as Greece, Italy and Spain, have 50 to 70 per cent less heart disease than the UK. Southern Europeans eat mainly unsaturates in their diet. Red meat is only eaten a few times a month, on special occasions. Small amounts of fish, poultry and eggs are also eaten. They eat lots of starchy carbohydrates such as bread, pasta and potatoes and plenty of fresh fruit and vegetables. They cook with olive oil, which is high in monounsaturates, and eat monounsaturates and polyunsaturates in the form of nuts, seeds and oily fish.

Fish is good for the heart

Omega 3 fatty acids, which are found in fish oils, may help improve blood flow to the heart. Eating oily fish, such as mackerel, salmon or tuna, twice a week, will provide around 1 gram a day of Omega 3 fatty acids. This may prevent **blood clots** forming and protect against heart disease.

Who has a good diet?

The Japanese diet contains just over 30 per cent fat, compared with 40 per cent in the UK and 55 per cent in Denmark. Japanese cooking is based on rice, fresh vegetables and oily fish, which are all rich in polyunsaturated fatty acids. Japan has one of the lowest rates of heart disease in the world. The Inuit people of Greenland also have a low rate of heart disease. Their diet is based on fish and marine animals, which are low in saturated fat and high in Omega 3 fatty acids.

Asian diets are based on foods that are high in starchy carbohydrates and low in fat.

Getting enough fat

Eating too much fatty food is bad for your health, but not eating any fat would stop the body getting important **nutrients**. We must eat some fat to get the essential **fatty acids**, which the body cannot make itself. Deficiency in these fatty acids can cause growth problems, arthritis and other health problems.

Omega 6 fatty acids

We need **Omega 6 fatty acids** to build healthy **cell** walls and make **hormones** and chemicals that control body processes like blood flow. Some people can have an Omega 6 deficiency because their bodies are not able to absorb fats properly. We need to eat about 4 grams of Omega 6 fatty acids a day. This is about two teaspoons of sunflower oil, or a few almonds or walnuts.

We also need about 1 to 2 grams of **Omega 3 fatty acids** a day, which is about 100 grams of oily fish, or two teaspoons of linseed oil. Omega 3 fatty acids are needed when the body is growing, to build healthy brain and eye tissue and to keep blood flowing properly.

You can buy a variety of low fat dairy products.

Fat for vitamins

The body needs some fat each day to provide and absorb enough of the **fat-soluble vitamins** A, D, E and K. When fats are removed from dairy products to make low fat products like yoghurts, skimmed milk and cottage cheese, these foods lose much of their vitamin A content. The body can make extra vitamin A from beta-carotene, which is found in leafy green and orange vegetables and orange and yellow fruits. But it needs fats in the diet to be able to absorb beta-carotene and fat-soluble vitamins.

Fats and growth

Fats are needed to help babies grow properly, and also during **puberty** when the body is growing rapidly. A baby grows to three times its birth weight in its first year. Fat is a natural part of breast milk. It provides around half the total daily intake of **kilojoules** until the baby is about one year old and starts eating solid foods.

Babies should not be fed cow's milk until after one year. They should have special formula milk or breast milk. Children under the age of two years should drink whole milk, after which semi-skimmed milk may be introduced. Skimmed milk is not suitable for children under five.

Babies need to drink full fat milk until they are about two years old. Solids, like prepared baby foods, eventually take the place of the liquid diet.

Balancing fats in the diet

A healthy diet needs to be low in **saturates** and have a good balance of **unsaturates**, including **Omega 6** and **Omega 3 fatty acids**. But in western countries like the UK and Australia, most of the fats in our diet are saturates from red meat, dairy products and sweets.

Health recommendations

Health experts recommend that most people in the UK reduce the amount of saturates from animal foods in their diet and increase the amounts of unsaturates from fish and plant foods. **Cholesterol** in the diet tends to be found in foods which are high in saturates.

We can get a healthy balance of fats in our diet by:
- using butter and spreads sparingly
- drinking semi-skimmed milk
- eating no more than three to four eggs a week
- eating less fatty meat and more oily fish
- cutting the fat off meat and skin off chicken
- avoiding too many fried foods like chips
- using olive oil or sunflower oil for cooking rather than hard fats, for example, butter or lard
- avoiding too many processed foods that contain saturated or **hydrogenated** fats.

We can also try to get a healthy balance of fats in our diet in the way we buy and cook our food.

Fats on food labels

Read food labels to check the fat content. UK food labels may list the total fat content per 100 grams or 100 millilitres, and the amount of saturates and unsaturates. They may also give the percentage of fat per 'serving' (such as a whole snack bar). Look for low levels of saturates and higher levels of unsaturates.

Cut down on fat by choosing lower fat foods. Compare the following to see what a difference it can make:

	100 grams of fried chips have 6.7 grams of fat
BUT	100 grams of jacket potatoes only contain 0.2 grams of fat.
	100 grams of roast beef contains 21 grams of fat
BUT	100 grams of roast chicken (without skin) only has 4 grams of fat.

Processed food

Seventy per cent of the fat that we eat is 'hidden' in processed foods. Try to avoid eating too many processed foods like cakes, crackers, snack bars and crisps. Lots of products that contain hydrogenated fats have had the **trans fats** removed.

We can try to balance our intake of higher fat foods with low fat foods to keep our total fat intake no more than 35 per cent each day. Look for low fat food products like semi-skimmed or skimmed milk, low fat yoghurt, oven chips or reduced fat cheese. But beware of labels claiming '90% fat free' – the product still contains 10 per cent fat!

Stir frying is a healthy way of cooking because it only uses small amounts of oil.

Low cholesterol foods

Some foods claim to lower blood cholesterol. They include fat and cheese spreads and yoghurts. They contain plant substances called plant sterols or plant stanol ester.

Cooking with fats

Choose healthy ways of cooking like grilling, steaming and baking, rather than frying and roasting. Stir-frying uses less fat than deep-frying. Hard fats such as lard and butter are high in saturates, so it is healthier to cook with vegetables oils such as olive oil or sunflower oil. Never re-use old cooking oil or eat burnt foods as they can contain the substances called **free radicals** which can damage your health.

Fats in the Balance of Good Health

A healthy diet is a balanced diet. It is made up of five main food groups. This chart shows the balance of foods from all five groups that we should eat daily.

Fruit and vegetables

Bread, other cereals and potatoes

Meat, fish, eggs and pulses

Fatty and sugary foods

Milk and dairy foods

Guidelines for healthy eating

Try to base main meals on starchy **carbohydrate** foods like pasta, rice and bread. Take **protein** from foods like chicken, fish, nuts and pulses. Boys aged twelve to fourteen need around 66 grams of protein a day; girls need around 53 grams of protein a day.

Eat at least five portions of fruit and vegetables in the diet each day. A portion is around 80 grams or:
• two serving spoons of carrots or spinach
• three serving spoons of peas or beans
• one apple, orange or banana
• ten strawberries
• three serving spoons of tinned fruit.

Eating a variety of fruits allows you to get the widest range of nutrients.

Try to include a variety of red fruits (for example, red grapes and berries) orange fruits and vegetables (oranges, carrots) and green fruits and vegetables (peas, beans, white grapes and so on).

Balance fats so you eat mainly **polyunsaturates** or **monounsaturates** from foods like oily fish, nuts, seeds and vegetable oils. Keep foods that are high in **saturates** like chips, cakes, and crisps as occasional treats.

Get a healthy balance

Fats have an important role to play in a healthy diet: there are 'good fats' as well as 'bad fats'. It is up to us to see that we get the balance right for our bodies.

Glossary

additive substance added to preserve or add flavour to food

amino acids parts of food that make up proteins and help break them down when food is being digested

antioxidant type of vitamin or substance believed to protect body cells from damage and ageing

artery blood vessel that carries blood from your heart

atom smallest part of any chemical

bacteria tiny living organism; some are helpful in the body, but others can be harmful

basal metabolic rate (BMR) energy we use each minute for basic body processes

bile substance made in the liver that helps break down fats

blood clot thick mass of blood that can block arteries

carbohydrates part of food which we need for energy

carbon simple chemical substance that is part of the make-up of fatty acids

cardiovascular having to do with the heart and the blood system

cell smallest unit of a plant or animal

chemical reaction when two or more chemicals react together to produce a change

cholesterol substance made by the body and found in some foods

developed countries mostly western countries that have well established industries and services, such as transport, schools and welfare

diabetes disease where the body cannot control the level of sugar in the blood

digestive system parts of the body that work to process food

dissolve to break down in water

emulsification process of breaking down fat so it can dissolve in water

energy power to be physically and mentally active

enzymes chemical agents that change food into substances we can absorb

essential fatty acids (EFAs) fatty acids that the body needs but can only get from food

ethanol type of alcohol

fat-soluble can dissolve in fats

fatty acid molecule made from a chain of carbon and hydrogen atoms, with one oxygen atom attached

fibre part of food which we need for healthy digestion

free radicals chemical substances which may harm health

gene information in the form of a body chemical, DNA, which carries the instructions for a living thing to develop and survive. These chemical instructions are inherited from parents.

germ (of wheat or corn) central part of grain which contains oil

glucose type of sugar made from carbohydrate and broken down in muscles to give energy

glycerol simple substance that is part of the make-up of fats

glycogen form in which glucose is stored in muscles

HDL cholesterol fatty substance carried in the blood by 'high density lipoproteins' that help reduce risk of heart disease

hormones chemicals made by cells in the body and carried by the blood

husk dry outer coating of a seed

hydrogen simple chemical substance that is part of the make-up of fatty acids

hydrogenation process used to make fats solid

immune system body's defences against germs and diseases

immunized protected against disease by a vaccination

insoluble cannot be dissolved in water

insulin type of hormone produced by the pancreas to control the amount of sugar in the blood

kilojoules (kJ) unit of energy in food

LDL cholesterol fatty substance carried in the blood by 'low density lipoproteins'. A large amount circulating in the blood increases the risk of heart disease.

liver organ in the body used in the digestive system. It makes bile and helps clean the blood.

lymphatic system liquid system that carries substances round the body and clears away waste matter

metabolic rate speed at which your body's chemical reactions occur

minerals nutrients found in foods that the body needs to stay healthy

molecule simple unit of a chemical substance

monounsaturated fatty acid which has one pair of hydrogen atoms missing

nutrients substances that the body needs to stay healthy

obesity when the BMI is 30 or above

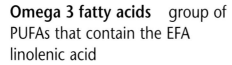

Omega 3 fatty acids group of PUFAs that contain the EFA linolenic acid

Omega 6 fatty acids group of PUFAs that contain the EFA linoleic acid

organs parts inside the body that have a special job to do

oxidize combine with oxygen to make an oxide

oxygen colourless gas needed for animals and plants to live

pancreas gland that makes insulin and enzymes to digest food

polyunsaturated fatty acid which has more than one pair of hydrogen atoms missing

polyunsaturated fatty acids (PUFAs) fatty acids that the body makes or has to get from food

protein part of food that we need for growth and energy

puberty time when a child's body matures so he or she is capable of having children

saliva fluid made by glands in the mouth and needed to digest food

saturated fatty acid that is saturated with hydrogen atoms

solution liquid that has a substance dissolved in it

soluble can dissolve in water

stroke sudden change in blood supply to the brain which can cause loss of movement in parts of the body

toxins poisonous substances

trans fats type of fat made by hydrogenation

triglycerides chemical form in which fats exist in foods and in the body

unsaturated fatty acid that is not saturated with hydrogen atoms

virus tiny living organism that can cause disease

vitamins nutrients found in food that we need to stay healthy

Resources

Books

Food and Nutrition, Anita Tull (OUP, 1996)

Food Values: Fats and Cholesterol, Patty Brian (HarperCollins, 1992)

Role of Fats in Food and Nutrition, Michael Gurr (Chapman and Hall, 1992)

Trends in Food Technology: Food Ingredients, Hazel King (Heinemann Library, 2002)

Trends in Food Technology: Food Processing, Anne Barnett (Heinemann Library, 2002)

Websites

www.bbc.co.uk/health/nutrition
Nutrition and healthy living are the subject of this part of the BBC's website.

www.bhf.org.uk/
Website for the British Heart Foundation.

www.fooddirectory.co.uk
Educational site set up by the Food Foundation.

www.nutrition.org.uk
Website for British Nutrition Foundation.

www.nutritionaustralia.org
The Australian Nutrition Foundation's website.

Index